DI
QU

C000292095

Over 200 questions and answers to help
you pass the written Theory Test

by

Jenny Robbins
D.O.T.A.D.I., Dip. D.I., Cert. Ed. (F.E.), M.I.A.M.

and

Peter Robbins
D.O.T.A.D.I., Dip. D.I., Cert. Ed. (F.E.), M.I.A.M.
DIAmond Advanced Examiner/Instructor

Shaw & Sons

Published by
Shaw & Sons Limited
Shaway House
21 Bourne Park
Bourne Road
Crayford
Kent DA1 4BZ

© Shaw & Sons Limited 1996

ISBN 0 7219 1047 5

First edition 1986
Revised reprint 1987
Second edition 1990
Revised reprint 1991
Revised reprint 1993
Third edition 1996

A CIP catalogue record for this book is available from the
British Library

Printed in Great Britain

CONTENTS

About this Book 4

About the Theory Test 4

How to Pass the Theory Test 5

OVER 200 MULTIPLE CHOICE QUESTIONS
AND ANSWERS 6

The Driving Test 66

Driving Tuition 79

Driving Instructor Associations 80

ABOUT THIS BOOK

This book has been written for learner drivers wanting an easy way to test their knowledge for the THEORY TEST and DRIVING TEST. The questions cover all the topics in the Theory Test and appear with multiple-choice answers below them.

The correct answers are revealed at the bottom of the following right-hand page, making them quick and easy to check. **In each question there is one correct answer unless otherwise stated.**

At the end of the book detailed information is given about all aspects of the driving test, including how the examiner marks the test and the standard of driving required to pass.

ABOUT THE THEORY TEST

You have 40 minutes to answer 35 multiple choice questions and it is in your interest to answer all of them. The questions test hazard awareness in specific driving situations, common sense, the Highway Code, vehicle handling characteristics, accident procedure and road safety.

You must have a U.K. provisional licence before you can apply and it must be produced when you take the test.

Tests will be offered within two weeks of applying and are available weekdays, evenings and Saturdays.

You may have to travel further to take the Theory Test than the Driving Test as there are far fewer centres.

Special needs such as dyslexia and other disabilities are catered for and the tests are being printed in Welsh and six ethnic languages.

The result of your test will be sent to you within 14 days.

HOW TO PASS THE THEORY TEST

Study the Highway Code.

Learn to drive before you apply to take the Theory Test. Some of the questions will assess your knowledge of the Driving Test manoeuvres and the correct use of car controls. You will be much more likely to pass the Theory Test when you have the practical experience of a wide variety of driving situations and you have developed your driving skills with an Approved Driving Instructor.

Many schools and colleges are offering training courses but at present any unqualified person can give training for the Theory Test so look for driving instructor qualifications (Approved Driving Instructor) and teacher qualifications (Certificate of Education).

Use *Driving Test Questions and Answers* to test your knowledge of all the topics included in the Theory Test.

1. **How much room should a driver leave when passing a parked vehicle?**
   (a) Enough room for two wing mirrors to pass.
   (b) Two feet.
   (c) Enough space for a door to open.
   (d) One metre.

2. **What does this warning sign mean?**
   (red border)
   (a) Two-way traffic crosses one-way road.
   (b) Traffic passing with equal priority.
   (c) Two-way traffic straight ahead.
   (d) End of one-way street.

3. **What are the legal alcohol limits for driving?**
   Two answers.
   (a) 35 mg of alcohol per 100 ml of breath.
   (b) 35 mg of alcohol per 100 ml of blood.
   (c) 80 mg of alcohol per 100 ml of breath.
   (d) 80 mg of alcohol per 100 ml of blood.

4. **When is it safe to beckon a pedestrian across the road?**
   (a) At a pedestrian crossing.
   (b) At a pelican crossing.
   (c) Never.
   (d) When the traffic has stopped.

5. **What does this motorway sign mean?** *(white lights on black background)*

- (a) End of temporary restriction.
- (b) End of speed limit.
- (c) No entry.
- (d) No stopping.

6. **How does a driver know when an indicator bulb has failed?**

- (a) A buzzer sounds.
- (b) The indicators do not work.
- (c) The indicator warning light flashes faster.
- (d) The battery warning light shows.

7. **What precautions should be taken by a driver parking a car on a slope?** *Two answers.*

- (a) Apply the hand brake and turn the steering wheel into the kerb.
- (b) Leave the car in gear, reverse if facing downhill and first if facing uphill.
- (c) Park against the kerb with the nearside wheels on the pavement.
- (d) Place a warning triangle at the back of the vehicle.

Answers to these questions appear at the foot of page 9.

8. **What does this sign mean?** *(yellow border, green background, white letter)*

   (a) Roundabout ahead.
   (b) Ring road.
   (c) Restaurant.
   (d) Recreation area.

9. **When would an examiner refuse to conduct a driving test?** *Three answers.*

   When the candidate :
   (a) Had an unsigned driving licence.
   (b) Produced a passport instead of a driving licence.
   (c) Showed a driving licence issued in another country.
   (d) In heavy traffic.

10. **What parts of a vehicle must be kept clean?** *Three answers.*

    (a) Lights.
    (b) Mirrors.
    (c) Tyres.
    (d) Windows.

11. **Which lane should be used when travelling at 70 mph on a three lane motorway?**

    (a) The centre lane.
    (b) The fast lane.
    (c) The right-hand lane.
    (d) The left-hand lane unless overtaking.

12. What does this sign mean? *(blue background, white markings, red diagonal line)*

(a) End of dual carriageway.
(b) End of motorway.
(c) End of two-way traffic.
(d) Start of one-way system.

13. What is a safe time-gap between two vehicles on a dry day in good conditions?

(a) 3 seconds.
(b) 1 second.
(c) 2 seconds.
(d) 4 seconds.

14. What sort of signs are these?
(red borders)

(a) Mandatory signs.
(b) Prohibitive signs.
(c) Information signs.
(d) Warning signs.

Answers to questions on previous pages: 1–c; 2–c;
3–a, d; 4–c;
5–a; 6–c;
7–a, b.

9

15. How are stopping distances affected by wet weather?

(a) Stopping distances are not affected.
(b) Stopping distances are doubled.
(c) The brakes are less efficient.
(d) The driver must brake more quickly.

16. What action should you take if you miss your motorway exit?

(a) Leave by the next exit.
(b) Reverse back to it.
(c) Do a U-turn when the road is clear.
(d) Pull up on the hard shoulder.

17. What should you do if dazzled by the headlights of an oncoming vehicle?

(a) Switch your lights on main beam.
(b) Flash your lights to alert the driver.
(c) Slow down and be ready to stop if necessary.
(d) Speed up to pass the vehicle as soon as possible.

18. What does this warning sign mean?
(red border)

(a) Quayside or river bank.
(b) Level crossing.
(c) Opening or swing bridge ahead.
(d) Road liable to flood.

19. **On what side of the road are warning posts with red reflectors?**

    (a) On the left-hand side.
    (b) On the right-hand side.
    (c) On either side.
    (d) Approaching bends.

20. **What is the overall stopping distance of a car travelling at 60 mph in good conditions?**

    (a) 36 metres
    (b) 53 metres.
    (c) 73 metres.
    (d) 96 metres.

21. **When may a driver stop a vehicle on a yellow box junction?**

    (a) To allow traffic to emerge from a side road.
    (b) When the way ahead is blocked.
    (c) When turning left and waiting for turning traffic.
    (d) When turning right and waiting for oncoming traffic.

Answers to questions on previous pages: 8–b; 9–a, b, c;
10–a, b, d;
11–d; 12–b;
13–c; 14–d.

22. What warning does this sign give?

(black sign, white arrows)

- (a) Turn left.
- (b) Sharp deviation of route to left.
- (c) Double bends to left.
- (d) Temporary diversion.

23. What is the legal minimum tread depth for tyres?

- (a) 0.5 millimetre.
- (b) 1 millimetre.
- (c) 1.6 millimetres.
- (d) 3 millimetres.

24. What are the legal requirements for tyres? *Three answers.*

- (a) To be inflated to the correct pressure as recommended by the manufacturer.
- (b) To be fitted to wheels that are correctly balanced.
- (c) To have no cuts, bulges or splits.
- (d) To have tread depth not below the minimum legal requirements.

25. How would a driver exit from a motorway to visit a town on the right?

- (a) By the nearest Services.
- (b) By a slip road on the left.
- (c) By a slip road on the right.
- (d) By a flyover.

26. What does this road sign mean to the driver of a car? *(white background, black bar)* ***Two answers.***

(a) 70 mph on motorways and dual carriageways.

(b) 70 mph on motorways and 60 mph on dual carriageways.

(c) 60 mph on single carriageways unless otherwise indicated.

(d) 50 mph on single carriageways

27. What are the first two actions a driver must take if an accident occurs ahead? ***Two answers.***

(a) Call the emergency services.

(b) Stop in a safe place.

(c) Warn other traffic.

(d) Take details of the vehicles involved.

28. What is the correct way to drive through flood water safely?

(a) Slowly in first gear using the foot brake.

(b) In second gear accelerating gently.

(c) In a low gear, not making waves.

(d) In first gear slipping the clutch to keep engine speed high.

Answers to questions on previous pages: 15–b; 16–a; 17–c; 18–c; 19–a; 20–c; 21–d.

29. **What does a flashing amber light on a vehicle signify?** *Two answers.*

   (a) A tram.
   (b) A school bus.
   (c) A breakdown vehicle.
   (d) A slow moving vehicle such as a tractor.

30. **What is the final action a driver should take before altering direction or moving off from a parked position?**

   (a) Adjust the mirror.
   (b) Select first gear.
   (c) Look round to check blind spots.
   (d) Signal.

31. **What must a driver do before leaving a vehicle parked on the road?**

   (a) Check the doors are locked.
   (b) Turn off the lights.
   (c) Switch off the engine.
   (d) Keep off yellow parking restrictions.

32. **What driving manoeuvres are illegal within the zig-zag lines of a pedestrian crossing?** *Two answers.*

   (a) U-turns.
   (b) Overtaking the leading vehicle.
   (c) Parking.
   (d) Accelerating.

33. Which rule applies when parking in fog?

(a) Leave the rear fog light on.
(b) Leave the side lights on.
(c) Park facing towards the traffic.
(d) Place a warning triangle to the rear of the car.

34. When should dim-dipped headlights be used? *Two answers.*

(a) In fog.
(b) In drizzly weather conditions.
(c) At night where street lighting is bright.
(d) In heavy rain.

35. When must a driver stop at a pedestrian crossing?

(a) When pedestrians are waiting to cross.
(b) When pedestrians are on the crossing.
(c) When pedestrians are approaching a crossing.
(d) Drivers have right of way and do not have to stop.

36. What does this sign mean? *(red border)*

(a) Road narrows on both sides.
(b) Dual carriageway ends.
(c) Bottle-neck ahead.
(d) Single lane traffic ahead.

Answers to questions on previous pages: **22–b; 23–c;
24–a, c, d;
25–b; 26–a, c;
27–b, c; 28–d.**

37. What does this motorway sign mean?
(white lights, two amber flashing lights)

    (a) Right-hand lane closed ahead.
    (b) Speed restriction in right-hand lane.
    (c) No overtaking.
    (d) No through road ahead.

38. When may hazard warning lights be used on a moving vehicle?

    (a) When the indicators are not working.
    (b) When a vehicle is being towed.
    (c) To warn of a hazard ahead on a motorway.
    (d) When you intend to park in a restricted parking zone.

39. What is the minimum number of mirrors a private car must have?

    (a) Interior mirror and off-side wing mirror.
    (b) Interior mirror only.
    (c) Interior mirror and off-side and near-side wing mirrors.
    (d) Interior mirror and near-side mirror.

40. What does this sign mean? *(red background, white lettering)*

    (a) Stop if traffic on major road.
    (b) Stop, and give way.
    (c) Stop if pedestrians crossing.
    (d) Stop.

41. What direction should a parked vehicle face at night?

(a) Either direction.
(b) Facing oncoming traffic.
(c) Facing the same way as the traffic flow.
(d) On the right-hand side of the road.

42. What rules apply to a driver supervising a learner driver? *Two answers.*

The supervising driver must:
(a) Have held a full driving licence for a minimum of two years.
(b) Have held a full driving licence for a minimum of three years.
(c) Have passed an advanced driving test.
(d) Be twenty-one years of age or over.

43. What action must be taken if a car starts to skid during braking?

(a) Release the brake pedal.
(b) Steer into the skid.
(c) Accelerate briskly.
(d) Apply the hand brake.

Answers to questions on previous pages: 29–c, d; 30–c;
31–c; 32–b, c;
33–b; 34–b, c;
35–b; 36–a.

44. What does this sign mean? *(red border)*

- (a) Sharp bend to the left.
- (b) Hills ahead.
- (c) Uneven road surface.
- (d) Double bend (first to the left).

45. What documents does a car require? *Four answers.*

- (a) Vehicle excise licence (tax disc) unless the car is over 25 years old.
- (b) Motor insurance.
- (c) M.O.T. Certificate when the car is three years old.
- (d) Service records.
- (e) Registration document.

46. Why is extra care needed by a driver intending to pass oncoming traffic nearside to nearside when turning right?

- (a) The traffic situation may change.
- (b) An approaching vehicle can obstruct the driver's view of oncoming traffic.
- (c) The driver may have to wait in the centre of the junction.
- (d) Other drivers may not see the driver's signal.

47. What is the meaning of amber flashing lights at a pelican crossing? *Two answers.*

(a) Drivers must give way to pedestrians on the crossing.
(b) Drivers must stop until the green light shows.
(c) Drivers must stop.
(d) Drivers may drive on when there are no pedestrians on the crossing.

48. What action would you take if the word FOG appeared on a motorway sign but the road ahead was clear?

(a) Drive very slowly.
(b) Be prepared for drifting fog.
(c) Proceed as normal.
(d) Leave at the next exit.

49. What does this road sign mean? *(red border)*

(a) No motor vehicles.
(b) No vehicles.
(c) No entry.
(d) No parking.

Answers to questions on previous pages: 37–a; 38–c; 39–a; 40–b; 41–c; 42–b, d; 43–a.

50. **How do police in a police car signal a driver to pull over?**

   (a) Flashing blue light.
   (b) Flashing blue light and siren.
   (c) Flashing blue light, siren and hazard warning lights.
   (d) Flashing blue light, left indicator flashing and 'point' to the left.

51. **What is meant by the 'rule of the road' on motorways?**

   (a) Drive in the left-hand lane unless overtaking or signs direct otherwise.
   (b) Use the right-hand lane for cruising.
   (c) Drive in the middle lane. The left-hand lane is for lorries and coaches.
   (d) Drive in the middle lane and use the right-hand lane for overtaking.

52. **When should rear fog lights be used?**

   (a) In fog and mist.
   (b) To prevent traffic following too closely.
   (c) When visibility is below 100 metres.
   (d) When parking in fog.

53. **What does this road sign mean?** *(red border, black car/red car)*

   (a) No overtaking.
   (b) Two lanes of traffic.
   (c) Start of two-way traffic.
   (d) Dual carriageway ahead.

54. Assuming your journey is essential, how should you drive in snow?

(a) In a high gear and slip the clutch.
(b) Slowly in as low a gear as possible.
(c) Slowly in as high a gear as possible.
(d) Stay in first gear.

55. What does it mean if a traffic controller facing you raises the right arm?

(a) You may turn right only.
(b) You may turn left only.
(c) Traffic behind the controller must stop.
(d) You must stop.

56. What action would you take if your engine stopped on a level crossing?

(a) Keep trying to start the car.
(b) Get yourself and passengers out to a place of safety.
(c) Try to push the car off the railway lines.
(d) Stay in the car.

Answers to questions on previous pages: 44–d;
45–a, b, c, e;
46–b; 47–a, d;
48–b; 49–b.

57. Who would carry a white stick with two reflective bands?

(a) A deaf person.
(b) A blind person.
(c) A deaf and blind person.
(d) A pedestrian at night.

58. What does this road sign mean? *(red border)*

(a) Warning cyclists.
(b) Cycle route only.
(c) No cycling.
(d) Cycle lane.

59. Where can drivers stop and park on a motorway, for example if tired?

(a) Service area.
(b) Hard shoulder.
(c) Slip road.
(d) Left-hand lane.

60. What is the next traffic light signal after a red light?

(a) Amber.
(b) Red and amber.
(c) Flashing amber.
(d) Green.

61. What is the meaning of a red and amber traffic light signal?

(a) Stop.
(b) Go if clear.
(c) Stop unless you have crossed the line.
(d) Get ready to go.

62. What does this road sign mean? *(red border)*

(a) No entry.
(b) No left turn ahead.
(c) Turn left ahead.
(d) No left turn.

63. What separation distance should you leave between your vehicle and other traffic on a dry day when travelling at 20 mph?

(a) 6 metres.
(b) 12 metres.
(c) 18 metres.
(d) 23 metres.

Answers to questions on previous pages: **50–d; 51–a; 52–c; 53–a; 54–c; 55–d; 56–b.**

64. You are approaching a level crossing. What do red or amber lights mean?

(a) Proceed with caution.
(b) Give way to trains on the crossing.
(c) Go if the train has passed.
(d) Stop.

65. When should a driver use dipped headlights during the daytime? *Two answers.*

(a) Dull conditions.
(b) Poor visibility.
(c) Fog.
(d) When it is frosty.

66. What does this sign mean? *(red border, small arrow red, large arrow black)*

(a) Give way to oncoming vehicles.
(b) Your priority.
(c) Two way traffic ahead.
(d) Road narrows.

67. What rules apply regarding loads carried in or on a car? *Two answers.*

(a) Headlights should be checked and realigned if necessary.
(b) The load should be checked at regular intervals during the journey.
(c) The load must be lightened whenever possible.
(d) The load must be evenly distributed and securely fastened.

68. **What are the first three actions a driver should take if a car breaks down or has a puncture on a motorway?** *Three answers.*

  (a) Ring for assistance from the nearest emergency telephone then wait near the car for the breakdown vehicle.

  (b) Get pets out of the vehicle and try and keep them away from the carriageway.

  (c) Stop on the hard shoulder as far from the carriageway as possible and switch on the hazard warning lights.

  (d) Look under the bonnet to try and identify the fault before the arrival of the breakdown vehicle, or change the wheel yourself.

  (e) Passengers should exit from doors away from the carriageway and wait well back from the motorway.

69. **What does a flashing green light on a vehicle signify?**

  (a) Trainee ambulance driver.

  (b) Doctor on an emergency call.

  (c) Tractor carrying farm chemicals.

  (d) Bomb disposal unit.

Answers to questions on previous pages: ***57–c; 58–c; 59–a; 60–b; 61–a; 62–d; 63–b.***

70. **What does this road sign mean?** *(red border, black figures)*

   (a) Children playing in road.
   (b) Pedestrian crossing ahead.
   (c) Children going to or from school or playground.
   (d) Amusement park.

71. **What does this sign mean?** *(red circle)* ***Two answers.***

   (a) You are entering a 20 mph zone.
   (b) You are entering a residential area and there may be children crossing.
   (c) You are entering an urban clearway.
   (d) Waiting restricted to 20 minutes only.

72. **What does this road sign mean?** *(blue background, white arrows)*

   (a) Drivers may pass either side.
   (b) Drivers can turn left or right.
   (c) One way street ahead.
   (d) Road works.

73. **What should a driver do when being overtaken by another vehicle?**

   (a) Slow down to let the vehicle pass.
   (b) Do not increase speed. Allow the overtaking vehicle to pass.
   (c) Speed up.
   (d) Keep a steady speed and signal the driver to pass.

74. **What is the overall stopping distance of a car travelling at 30 mph in good conditions?**

   (a) 36 metres.
   (b) 6 metres.
   (c) 12 metres.
   (d) 23 metres.

75. **When is it illegal to sound the horn of a vehicle?** *Two answers.*

   (a) Between 11.30 pm and 7.30 am (2330-0730) in a built up area.
   (b) Between 11.00 pm and 7.00 am (2300-0700) in a built up area.
   (c) Between 11.30 pm and 7.00 am (2330-0700) in a built up area.
   (d) When a vehicle is stopped unless in danger from a moving vehicle.

76. **What does this sign mean?** *(yellow sign, black border and figures)* **Two answers.**

   (a) Be prepared, children may be crossing.
   (b) School bus stop.
   (c) School entrance.
   (d) School bus.

Answers to questions on previous pages: **64–d; 65–b, c; 66–a; 67–a, d; 68–a, c, e; 69–b.**

77. How would a driver release the steering lock on a car?

(a) Unlock the driver's door.
(b) Insert the ignition key and turn while trying to turn the steering wheel.
(c) Start the car and hold the wheel tightly.
(d) Turn the ignition key both ways.

78. What does this road sign mean? *(red border)*

(a) No pedestrians.
(b) Pedestrians crossing.
(c) No footpath ahead.
(d) Pedestrians only.

79. When should a driver *not* stop at an amber traffic light signal? *Two answers.*

(a) When the lights change unexpectedly.
(b) When the vehicle is going too fast.
(c) When the vehicle has already crossed the STOP line.
(d) When the vehicle is so close to the line that to pull up might cause an accident.

80. Where would you see warning posts with white reflectors?

(a) On the right-hand side of the carriageway.
(b) On the left-hand side of the carriageway.
(c) On either side of the carriageway.
(d) At a STOP junction.

81. What action should a driver take when another vehicle is following too closely on a motorway?

  (a) Reduce speed gradually by easing off the accelerator.

  (b) Touch the brakes to flash the brake lights.

  (c) Slow down and wave the driver on.

  (d) Speed up.

82. Where is it illegal to park?

  (a) On a dual carriageway

  (b) 15 metres from a road junction.

  (c) Where there is a solid white line in the centre of the road.

  (d) On the right-hand side of a one-way street.

83. How should you signal and position your vehicle to follow the road ahead at a roundabout? *(red border)*

  (a) Signal left on approach and stay in the left lane.

  (b) No signal on approach. Stay in the left lane and signal left to exit.

  (c) Signal right and use right lane. Signal left to exit.

  (d) No signal and either lane on approach. Signal left to exit.

Answers to questions on previous pages: **70–c; 71–a, b; 72–a; 73–b; 74–d; 75–c, d; 76–a, d.***

84. **Why must care be taken before opening a car door?** *Two answers.*

    (a) It is an offence to endanger other road users.

    (b) To protect the car door.

    (c) To prevent injury to a pedestrian or cyclist.

    (d) A stranger might get in the car.

85. **What is the purpose of a motorway acceleration lane?**

    (a) To park prior to joining the carriageway in a suitable gap.

    (b) To adjust the speed of a vehicle to join the carriageway in a suitable gap.

    (c) To wait for a gap at the start of the acceleration lane then join the carriageway.

    (d) To increase the speed of your vehicle and make the traffic move over.

86. **Where are the red coloured studs on motorways and dual carriageways?**

    (a) On the left side of the carriageway.

    (b) On the right side of the carriageway.

    (c) In the centre of the carriageway.

    (d) On either side of the carriageway.

87. **What does this road sign mean?** *(blue background, white arrows)*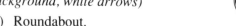

    (a) Roundabout.

    (b) The road curves round to the right.

(c) One-way system ahead.

(d) Mini-roundabout.

88. How far apart are the countdown markers to motorway exits?

(a) 30, 20, 10 yards before an exit.

(b) One mile, half a mile, quarter of a mile before an exit.

(c) 250, 150, 50 yards before an exit.

(d) 300, 200,100 yards before an exit.

89. When must a driver not reverse? *Two answers.*

(a) Into a side road.

(b) Out of a side road.

(c) Out of a main road.

(d) For longer than necessary.

90. When should tyre pressures be checked?

(a) After a long journey.

(b) Before filling up with fuel.

(c) After the tyres have cooled.

(d) Only by a qualified mechanic.

Answers to questions on previous pages: 77–b; 78–a; 79–c,d; 80–a; 81–a; 82–c; 83–b.

91. What does this road sign mean? *(red border)*

    (a) No overtaking.
    (b) No motor vehicles.
    (c) Motorcycle track ahead.
    (d) No vehicles.

92. When should arm signals be used?

    (a) On a sunny day.
    (b) When the indicators are not working.
    (c) To confirm a right turn after passing a parked vehicle.
    (d) When driving across a pedestrian crossing.

93. What does this arm signal mean?

    (a) A turning left arm signal.
    (b) A turning right arm signal.
    (c) To let a traffic controller know you are going ahead.
    (d) A slowing down arm signal.

94. What does this arm signal mean?

    (a) A turning left arm signal.
    (b) A turning right arm signal.
    (c) To let a traffic controller know you are going ahead.
    (d) A slowing down arm signal.

95. What does this road sign mean? *(red border)*

(a) A T-junction.

(b) A staggered junction.

(c) A side road on the right.

(d) Cross-roads.

96. Which of the following 'tram rules' is incorrect?

(a) Do not enter a road or lane reserved for trams.

(b) Drivers may park in areas used by trams.

(c) Diamond shaped signs are for tram drivers only.

(d) Give way to trams and do not overtake them.

97. When would it be an offence to overtake another vehicle? *Two answers.*

(a) In the zig-zag lines approaching a pedestrian crossing.

(b) On a clearway.

(c) When there is a solid white line on your side of the centre of the road.

(d) When there is a NO OVERTAKING sign.

Answers to questions on previous pages: **84–a, c; 85–b; 86–a; 87–d; 88–d; 89–b, d; 90–c.**

98. How much 'passing room' should a driver allow a cyclist?

(a) One metre.
(b) Enough room for the cyclist to fit through.
(c) Room for the pedals to turn safely.
(d) Enough room for the cyclist to wobble or fall without danger of a collision.

99. What does this road sign mean? *(red border)*

(a) Steep hill downwards.
(b) Steep hill upwards.
(c) Select a low gear.
(d) Test your brakes.

100. What vehicles are allowed to use the third right-hand lane on a motorway?

(a) Heavy goods vehicles under 7.5 tonnes.
(b) Coaches.
(c) Buses longer than 12 metres.
(d) Cars towing a trailer.

101. Which lane should be used for turning right out of a one-way street?

(a) The centre lane.
(b) The left-hand lane.
(c) The right-hand lane.
(d) No particular lane.

102. What part of the car is not inspected during the M.O.T. test?

(a) Windscreen wipers and washers.
(b) Radiator.
(c) Speedometer.
(d) Hand brake.

103. What is the significance of the END OF DUAL CARRIAGEWAY sign?

(a) There will be parked vehicles ahead.
(b) Traffic merges from the left.
(c) Drivers must adapt to a two-way traffic flow.
(d) Overtaking will be more hazardous.

104. What does this sign mean? *(red border)*

(a) Sharp deviation ahead.
(b) Road works.
(c) Diversion.
(d) Change to opposite carriageway.

Answers to questions on previous pages: ***91–b; 92–c;***
93–d; 94–a;
95–a; 96–b;
97–a, d *(not c*
unless the line
is crossed).

105. Which three people have the authority to stop or direct traffic? *Three answers.*

(a) Police.
(b) Council workman.
(c) Traffic warden.
(d) School crossing patrol with a STOP CHILDREN sign.

106. When does a bus driver have priority?

(a) At a bus stop.
(b) When signalling an intention to move off from a bus stop.
(c) At a pelican crossing.
(d) Pulling out at a road junction.

107. How far behind a vehicle should a warning triangle be placed on a single carriageway road?

(a) 50 metres.
(b) 75 metres.
(c) 100 metres.
(d) 25 metres.

108. How far behind a vehicle should a warning triangle be placed on a motorway?

(a) 50 metres.
(b) 100 metres.
(c) 150 metres.
(d) 200 metres.

109. What do red triangular signs mean?

- (a) Prohibitive sign.
- (b) Mandatory sign.
- (c) Information sign.
- (d) Warning sign.

110. Who is responsible for a child of under 14 years wearing a seat-belt?

- (a) The child.
- (b) The parents.
- (c) The driver and front seat passenger.
- (d) The driver.

111. What is the purpose of the right-hand lane on a dual carriageway? *Two answers.*

- (a) Turning right.
- (b) Overtaking.
- (c) Cruising.
- (d) To prevent bunching of vehicles.

112. What is the meaning of a green traffic light signal?

- (a) Go as soon as the green light shows.
- (b) Go, if the way is clear.
- (c) Go when you have looked both ways.
- (d) Go.

Answers to questions on previous pages: **98–d; 99–a;**
100–a; 101–c;
102–b; 103–c;
104–d.

113. What does this road sign mean? *(red border)*

(a) Farm entrance, beware animals crossing.

(b) Toll bridge.

(c) Level crossing with barrier or gate ahead.

(d) Road closed at night.

114. When is it safe for a driver to answer a hand-held telephone?

(a) In a bus lane.

(b) In a traffic jam.

(c) At motorway Services.

(d) On the hard shoulder of a motorway.

115. What precaution should a driver take after driving through flood water?

(a) Dry the windscreen.

(b) Check the fuel.

(c) Test the brakes.

(d) Use the wipers.

116. How can a driver dry the brakes of a vehicle after driving through water?

(a) Use a chamois leather cloth.

(b) Drive at high speed for one minute.

(c) Switch on the heater.

(d) Pump the brake pedal or drive resting the left foot on the brake pedal.

117.What is the shortest distance to stop a vehicle travelling at 50 mph?

- (a) 36 metres.
- (b) 53 metres.
- (c) 73 metres.
- (d) 96 metres.

118.What does this road sign mean? *(red border, red/amber/green lights)*

- (a) Temporary traffic lights.
- (b) Traffic signals.
- (c) Manual traffic signals ahead.
- (d) Failure of traffic signals.

119.What should a driver switch on in thick fog? *Three answers.*

- (a) Windscreen wipers.
- (b) Rear windscreen demister.
- (c) Heater.
- (d) Dipped headlights.
- (e) Fog lights.

Answers to questions on previous pages: ***105–a, c, d;***
106–b; 107–a;
108–c; 109–d;
110–d;111–a,b;
112–b.

120. What do these road markings mean?

(a) A driver must not park on either side of the road or cross the solid line if it is nearer the vehicle than the broken line.

(b) A driver must not park on the side of the road nearest the solid line or overtake if the solid line is on the side of the vehicle.

(c) A driver can cross the broken line if it is on the side of the vehicle, and may park on the left-hand side.

(d) A driver must not cross the solid line but may park when it is safe to do so.

121. What causes a skid?

(a) Ice on road.

(b) Wet weather.

(c) Driver error.

(d) Fallen leaves.

122. What does this road sign mean? *(red border)*

(a) Falling rocks.

(b) Slippery road surface.

(c) Loose chippings.

(d) Drive slowly.

123.When may a driver overtake on the left? *Three answers.*

   (a) When traffic is turning right.
   (b) To pass slower traffic.
   (c) Where a filter system is in operation.
   (d) When traffic is moving slowly in queues.

124.What do red flashing motorway lights mean?

   (a) Hazard ahead.
   (b) You must not go beyond the signal in that lane.
   (c) Slow down.
   (d) Stop when you see the stop sign.

125.How can a driver stop a vehicle safely in an emergency? *Two answers.*

   (a) Press the brake and clutch pedals quickly together.
   (b) Hold the wheel firmly and brake promptly but progressively.
   (c) Pull the hand brake on just before you stop.
   (d) Leave the clutch alone until the vehicle is almost stationary.

Answers to questions on previous pages: ***113–c; 114–c;***
115–c; 116–d;
117–b; 118–b;
119–a, d, e.

126. What does this sign mean? *(blue background, large white and small red arrow)*

   (a) Give way to oncoming vehicles.
   (b) One-way system ahead.
   (c) Stop and give way.
   (d) Priority over vehicles from opposite direction.

127. What should a driver do after stopping in a safe place when an accident has occurred ahead? *Three answers.*

   (a) Switch on hazard lights.
   (b) Move casualties away from the road.
   (c) Warn other traffic and switch off engines.
   (d) Assess the situation and alert the emergency services.

128. If you feel sleepy when driving on a motorway, what action should you take?

   (a) Stop on the hard shoulder and have a short nap.
   (b) Close your eyes every few seconds.
   (c) Listen to the radio.
   (d) Open the window and stop at the next Service area.

129. What do you do if a rear wheel skid occurs?

   (a) Accelerate into the skid
   (b) Turn the opposite way to the skid.
   (c) Turn into the skid.
   (d) Wait for the skid to stop.

130. What do these road markings at a roundabout mean?

(a) Give way to traffic on a major road.
(b) Give way to traffic from the right.
(c) You have priority when you approach these road markings.
(d) You must stop.

131. What are the legal eyesight requirements for a car driver? *Two answers.*

(a) Drivers who break their glasses are allowed to drive to an optician.
(b) A driver who needs glasses or lenses must wear them for driving.
(c) A driver must be able to read a number plate at 20.5 metres.
(d) A driver must be able to read a number plate at 35 metres.

132. What would be the overall stopping distance of a car travelling at 40 mph in wet conditions?

(a) 12 metres.
(b) 24 metres.
(c) 46 metres.
(d) 73 metres.

Answers to questions on previous pages: **120–a; 121–c;**
122–c;
123–a, c, d;
124–b; 125–b, d.

133. What should an alert driver be anticipating when driving past stationary buses or ice-cream vans?

    (a) Pedestrians can walk across to the vehicle.

    (b) The vehicle may move off.

    (c) A child might run out from behind the vehicle.

    (d) A door could open.

134. What does this road sign mean? *(blue circle, white arrow)*

    (a) Keep left.

    (b) Turn left.

    (c) Turn left ahead.

    (d) No left turn.

135. Which warning light warns of a fault that could cause an accident?

    (a) Seat belt warning light.

    (b) Hand brake warning light.

    (c) Ignition (battery warning) light.

    (d) Brake fluid level warning light.

136. When is it useful to change down a gear? *Two answers.*

    (a) To slow the car down.

    (b) To provide more power for the overtaking manoeuvre.

    (c) To increase control driving downhill.

    (d) To utilise engine braking before stopping.

137. What precautions should a driver take immediately before starting the engine?

Check:

(a) The hand brake is on and the gear lever is in neutral.

(b) The gear lever is in neutral and the hand brake is on.

(c) The mirrors are adjusted correctly.

(d) The doors are shut.

138. Why is it be dangerous to follow the tail lights of a vehicle in fog?

(a) The driver could be lost.

(b) The vehicle might stop suddenly.

(c) The rear lights are dazzling.

(d) The fog seems lighter because the leading vehicle is displacing it.

139. What is the routine all drivers should follow before any driving manoeuvre?

(a) Position, speed, look.

(b) Look, assess, decide.

(c) Mirrors, signal, manoeuvre.

(d) Brake, gear, accelerate.

Answers to questions on previous pages: ***126–d;***
127–a, c, d;
128–d; 129–c;
130–b;131–b,c;
132–d.

140. **What should you do if your car breaks down on the motorway and you are unable to get your vehicle on to the hard shoulder?**

   (a) Leave the vehicle and run across the carriageway.
   (b) Switch on hazard warning lights and stay in the vehicle if you cannot get clear of the carriageway safely.
   (c) Switch on hazard warning lights and flag down other drivers.
   (d) Stand on the central reservation.

141. **If a vehicle in front of you is carrying a hazardous load and has an accident, what should you do?**

   (a) Stay well back and alert the emergency services. Give details of the hazard information panel if possible but do not place yourself at risk to do so.
   (b) Go and see if you can help the driver.
   (c) Examine the load and inform the emergency services if it is dangerous.
   (d) Leave the scene of the accident immediately.

142. **What does it mean if amber lights flash and alarm bells ring when you are driving across a level crossing?**

   (a) Warning of a train approaching the crossing in five minutes.

(b) Stop and reverse back off the crossing to the 'give way' line.
(c) Get the passengers out and try to stop the train.
(d) Keep going if the vehicle is already on the crossing. Do not stop on the crossing.

143. What parking rules apply in a 30 mph speed limit?

(a) Vehicles must have side lights on.
(b) Vehicles do not need lights and can park on either side of the road.
(c) Vehicles do not need lights switched on and must face the same way as the traffic flow.
(d) Vehicles must have dipped headlights on and be parked on the left-hand side.

144. A driver must use the mirrors before: *Three answers.*

(a) Slowing and stopping.
(b) Starting the engine.
(c) Signalling.
(d) Changing direction and overtaking.

Answers to questions on previous pages: ***133–c; 134–a; 135–d; 136–b,c; 137–a; 138–b; 139–c.***

145. What does this sign mean? *(blue background, white arrow)*

(a) Ahead only.
(b) One-way traffic.
(c) Straight up.
(d) Turn left.

146. Where must a driver stop at a pedestrian crossing?

(a) At the give-way line one metre from the crossing.
(b) Within the zig-zag lines.
(c) With the front wheels of the car on the crossing.
(d) Two metres from the crossing.

147. What would be the likely cause of no current when an ignition key was turned in a vehicle?

(a) Wrong key.
(b) No fuel.
(c) Battery leads loose or disconnected.
(d) Car may have a time switch.

148. Why must a driver be careful to reduce speed when leaving a motorway?

(a) Motorway exit roads have a lower speed limit.
(b) Slower speeds will seem faster.
(c) To conserve fuel.
(d) Many motorway exits have sharp bends joining non-motorway roads.

149. What do these white diagonal stripes painted on the road mean?

(a) Never enter these areas.

(b) Do not drive over these areas unless it is safe to do so.

(c) Do not enter these areas when turning right.

(d) Keep off the hazard warning lines.

150. What vehicles are not allowed to use motorways? *Two answers.*

(a) Tractors and very slow moving vehicles.

(b) Wide loads.

(c) Motorcycles under 50cc.

(d) Snow ploughs.

151. What drivers are not allowed to drive on motorways? *Two answers.*

(a) Provisional licence holders.

(b) Drivers under 21 years.

(c) Drivers with less than two years' driving experience.

(d) Drivers of some invalid carriages.

Answers to questions on previous pages: **140–b; 141–a; 142–d; 143–c; 144–a, c, d.**

152. What should follow the mirrors, signal, manoeuvre routine?

(a) Right, left, right.
(b) Brake, gear, accelerate.
(c) Position, speed, look.
(d) Doors, seating, seat belt.

153. What should you do if a suitcase falls off your vehicle on to the motorway?

(a) Stop on the hard shoulder and pick up the suitcase and contents.
(b) Stop on the hard shoulder and use the emergency telephone.
(c) Drive on.
(d) Report the loss when you leave the motorway.

154. What should you do if the flashing blue lights of an emergency vehicle appear in your rear view mirror?

(a) Stop immediately.
(b) Allow the vehicle to pass when safe to do so. Do not stop suddenly.
(c) Drive on to the pavement and allow the vehicle to pass.
(d) Continue driving. The vehicle will overtake when ready to do so.

155. What does this sign mean?
(blue background, white bus and arrows)

- (a) Contra-flow bus lane.
- (b) With-flow bus lane.
- (c) Bus lane in operation.
- (d) Keep out of bus lanes.

156. What rule must drivers observe regarding bus lanes?

- (a) Never enter a bus lane.
- (b) Give way to buses in bus lanes.
- (c) Keep out of bus lanes during the times they are in operation.
- (d) Buses have priority in bus lanes.

157. By how much are stopping distances increased during icy weather?

- (a) Ten times.
- (b) Five times.
- (c) Three times.
- (d) Twice.

Answers to questions on previous pages: **145–b; 146–a; 147–c; 148–d; 149–b; 150–a, c; 151–a, d.**

158. What must a driver never do at an automatic half-barrier level crossing?

   (a) Wait until the train has passed before crossing.

   (b) Allow passengers to alight.

   (c) Wait with the engine running.

   (d) Zig-zag round the barriers.

159. What does this road sign mean? *(blue background, red border and cross)*

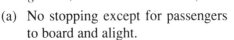

   (a) No stopping except for passengers to board and alight.

   (b) Clearway. A driver may not stop or park on the carriageway.

   (c) Parking allowed for a limited period only.

   (d) End of waiting restrictions.

160. What final check should a driver make before reversing, and why?

   (a) Look all round and behind the car and give way to pedestrians crossing.

   (b) Make sure the car is in reverse gear or you may drive forward.

   (c) Check the mirrors are adjusted correctly to see approaching traffic.

   (d) Check for children and wave them across the road if necessary.

161. What is the overall stopping distance of a vehicle travelling at 30 mph?

    (a) Nine car lengths.

    (b) Six car lengths.

    (c) 12 metres.

    (d) 36 metres.

162. Why might a cyclist giving a right arm signal on the approach to a roundabout keep in the left-hand lane?

    (a) The left-hand lane is a safer route for a cyclist and avoids crossing traffic lanes.

    (b) The cyclist doesn't know where he or she is going.

    (c) Lane discipline does not apply to cyclists.

    (d) The cyclist is nervous of traffic.

163. What do blue circular road signs mean?

    (a) Information signs

    (b) Warning signs.

    (c) Prohibitive signs

    (d) Mandatory signs.

Answers to questions on previous pages: **152–c; 153–b; 154–b; 155–a; 156–c; 157–a.**

164.You have been prescribed a course of medicine. What should you do if you are worried it could affect your driving?

(a) Stop taking the medicine.
(b) Do not drive until you have checked your medication with a pharmacist.
(c) Make an appointment to see your doctor.
(d) Drive more carefully until the course of medicine is finished.

165.It is dark. When should you use main-beam head-lights?

(a) On a clear road with street lights.
(b) On a road with no oncoming traffic and a 40 mph speed limit.
(c) On a clear road with a 30 mph speed limit.
(d) On a dual carriageway when there is no other traffic.

166.When would a driver use this arm signal?

(a) To signal to pedestrians at a pedestrian crossing.
(b) To warn a driver of an obstruction.
(c) To acknowledge the courtesy of another driver.
(d) To let a traffic controller know the intention is to go straight ahead.

167. What distance should be left between vehicles travelling at 70 mph?

(a) 36 metres.
(b) 96 metres.
(c) 73 metres.
(d) 53 metres.

168. You are approaching a roundabout. Who must you give way to?

(a) Traffic on the roundabout.
(b) Traffic approaching from the left.
(c) Traffic approaching from the immediate right.
(d) You have priority.

169. A new driver is much more likely to be involved in an accident. How can you reduce the chances of this happening?

(a) Take motorway tuition or Pass Plus lessons with an Approved Driving Instructor.
(b) Avoid driving on busy roads.
(c) Drive short journeys only until you have gained more experience.
(d) Keep within three miles of where you live for the first three months.

Answers to questions on previous pages: 158–d; 159–b; 160–a; 161–b; 162–a; 163–d.

170. What does a learner driver need in order to drive on the road? *Two answers.*

(a) Birth certificate.
(b) Comprehensive insurance cover.
(c) Valid signed provisional driving licence.
(d) Third party insurance cover.

171. What do these yellow lines mean?

(a) No parking.
(b) No loading or unloading.
(c) Parking restricted to short periods (see time plate).
(d) Waiting restricted to one hour only.

172. What should a driver do if a tyre bursts while driving?

(a) Stop quickly as in an emergency.
(b) Steer into the side of the road.
(c) Hold the wheel firmly and allow the car to roll to a halt.
(d) Use the gearbox to slow the car.

173. What parts of a vehicle is it essential to keep clean? *Two answers.*

(a) Tyres and spare wheel.
(b) Windscreen and windows.
(c) Lights, indicators and reflectors.
(d) Engine and battery.

174. When must a driver stop at a pedestrian crossing with a centre island?

(a) When a pedestrian on the pavement is waiting to cross.
(b) When a pedestrian is crossing the right-hand side of the crossing.
(c) When a pedestrian is crossing the left-hand side of the crossing.
(d) When a pedestrian is waiting on the island.

175. How far apart are the emergency telephones on a motorway?

(a) 100 metres.
(b) 500 metres.
(c) 1 mile.
(d) 2 miles.

176. Who has priority on a hill?

(a) Traffic driving uphill.
(b) Traffic driving downhill.
(c) Equal priority.
(d) The larger vehicle.

Answers to questions on previous pages: ***164–b; 165–d;***
166–d; 167–b;
168–c; 169–a.

177. What does this road sign mean? *(red border)*

- (a) Do not cross the white line in centre of the road.
- (b) Barrier ahead.
- (c) No vehicles.
- (d) No entry.

178. How should casualties be helped at the scene of a road accident? *Two answers.*

- (a) Move casualties carefully to the side of the road.
- (b) Do not move injured people.
- (c) Talk to casualties and keep them warm.
- (d) Give casualties a warm drink to prevent shock.

179. When should headlights be turned on? *Two answers.*

- (a) When visibility is poor.
- (b) At lighting up time.
- (c) When rush hour traffic is heavy.
- (d) When the road is icy.

180. What is the middle lane used for on a three lane single carriageway?

- (a) For faster drivers.
- (b) For overtaking or turning right according to road markings.
- (c) For use when traffic queues build up.
- (d) For emergency vehicles only.

181. **You are going to turn right at a cross-roads. An oncoming lorry is also approaching the cross-roads and signalling right. What should you do?**

(a) Turn right with care.
(b) Wait well back to allow for the larger turning circle of the lorry.
(c) Wait in the centre of the junction for the lorry to turn.
(d) Drive on and take the next turning on the right.

182. **When should police be notified after an accident involving a person or animal?**

(a) There is no need to notify the police.
(b) As soon as possible or within 24 hours.
(c) As soon as possible or within 48 hours.
(d) You must report the accident to the police within 7 days.

183. **What lights should a parked vehicle show in a built-up area at night?**

(a) No lights are required.
(b) Side lights.
(c) Side lights, registration plate lights and tail lights.
(d) Dipped headlights, registration plate lights.

Answers to questions on previous pages: ***170–c, d; 171–c;***
172–c; 173–b, c;
174–c; 175–c;
176–a.

184. What are the two main dangers at a road traffic accident?

- (a) Vehicles in the road and witnesses leaving the scene without giving details.
- (b) Further collision and fire.
- (c) Wrong or incomplete details being given to the emergency services.
- (d) People stopping to have a look and getting in the way.

185. What lane should be used by drivers going straight ahead at a roundabout?

- (a) Either lane on approach and the left-hand lane to exit.
- (b) The shortest route through the roundabout.
- (c) The right-hand lane on approach and the left-hand lane to exit.
- (d) The left-hand lane unless indicated by road markings or traffic conditions.

186. Where are motorway warning signals situated?

- (a) On the hard shoulder.
- (b) On the left-hand side of the carriageway.
- (c) At the service areas.
- (d) On the central reservation or an overhead gantry.

187. What does this sign mean? *(blue background and white numbers)*

(a) Minimum speed limit of 30 mph.

(b) Maximum speed limit of 30 mph.

(c) End of minimum speed limit.

(d) End of built-up area.

188. When should the hand brake be used?

(a) At a roundabout.

(b) At a GIVE WAY junction.

(c) At a STOP junction.

(d) At an uphill junction.

189. What is the routine for safe overtaking?

(a) Position, speed, look, mirrors, signal, manoeuvre.

(b) Mirrors, signal, manoeuvre, position, speed, look.

(c) Mirrors, signal, manoeuvre, speed, position, look.

(d) Mirrors, signal, manoeuvre, position, look speed.

Answers to questions on previous pages: ***177–d; 178–b,c;***
179–a,b; 180–b;
181–b; 182–b;
183–a.

190. What should a driver do if there are horses and riders on the road ahead?

- (a) Sound the horn to warn the riders and pass slowly.
- (b) Slow down and be prepared to stop if necessary.
- (c) Pass briskly and leave plenty of space as you pass.
- (d) Stop well back and wait until the riders have disappeared from view.

191. What does this motorway sign mean? *(black background, amber flashing lights)*

- (a) Leave at the next motorway exit.
- (b) Take the next turning on the left.
- (c) Turn left ahead.
- (d) Change lanes.

192. What do road signs in a red circle mean?

- (a) Mandatory.
- (b) Mostly prohibitive.
- (c) Warnings.
- (d) Primary route signs.

193. What do flashing headlights mean?

- (a) A warning only.
- (b) A signal to go.
- (c) Accident ahead.
- (d) A greeting.

194. When should a driver use the right-hand lane to leave a roundabout?

(a) To turn right.
(b) For overtaking slow moving vehicles.
(c) If you are uncertain of your exit.
(d) To go straight ahead.

195. What drivers do not have to wear a seat belt? *Two answers.*

(a) Small children.
(b) Pregnant women.
(c) Drivers holding an exemption certificate.
(d) Reversing drivers.

196. Light steering may be a warning of black ice or a sign the car is beginning to aquaplane on a wet road. What should a driver do?

(a) Reduce speed by easing off the accelerator.
(b) Change down through the gears.
(c) Brake sharply.
(d) Steer into the projected slide.

Answers to questions on previous pages: 184–b; 185–d; 186–d; 187–a; 188–c; 189–a.

197. Heavy steering pulling to one side in a vehicle could mean?

(a) Under-inflated (soft) tyre.
(b) Over-inflated tyre.
(c) Uneven weight distribution in car.
(d) Worn shock absorbers.

198. Where are the green studs on a motorway or dual carriageway?

(a) On the left-hand side of the carriageway.
(b) Marking acceleration and deceleration lanes.
(c) On the right-hand side of the carriageway.
(d) Service areas.

199. What colours are primary route signs?

(a) Blue and white.
(b) Brown and white.
(c) Black and white.
(d) Green and white with yellow route numbers.

200. When can a driver drive on at a red traffic light signal?

(a) When going in the direction shown by a green filter arrow.
(b) When you have already crossed the STOP line.
(c) When the way is clear.
(d) When there are no pedestrians on the crossing.

201. What do these yellow lines on the kerb mean?

(a) Hazard lines.
(b) Box junction.
(c) Parking restrictions.
(d) Loading restrictions.

202. Where would a driver see amber studs on a motorway or dual carriageway?

(a) Left-hand edge of the carriageway.
(b) Right-hand edge of the carriageway.
(c) Acceleration and deceleration lanes.
(d) Service areas.

Answers to questions on previous pages: **190–b; 191–d; 192–b; 193–a; 194–b; 195–c,d; 196–a.**

THE DRIVING TEST

Arrive in good time as the test may be cancelled if you are late. Your vehicle must be roadworthy and have regulation size L-plates that do not obscure the lights or windows. You must bring your U.K. provisional driving licence or the examiner will not conduct the test. The driving test takes about 40 minutes and the following exercises can be included; hill start, angle start, emergency stop, turn-in-the-road, reverse, reverse park. The examiner is there to assess your standard of driving and candidates must be able to drive confidently without instruction.

How the driving test is marked
On the examiner's Driving Test Report minor faults are entered with a dash and do not fail the candidate. Serious faults are marked with a X and dangerous faults are marked with a D. An X or D means a fail.

To ensure marking remains standard, a supervising examiner occasionally sits in the back of the car during a driving test.

Cockpit drill
The following 'cockpit drill' should be completed before driving: Doors, seating, mirrors, seat belts, fuel.

1. Comply with the requirements of the eyesight test

Before the driving test begins, the examiner asks the candidate to read a vehicle number plate at a distance of

20.5 metres. When a test candidate is unable to read the number plate due to defective eyesight, the examiner does not proceed with the test and the test fee is forfeited.

2. Take proper precautions before starting the engine

Make sure the hand brake is applied and the gear lever is in neutral before starting the engine.

3. Make proper use of:

Accelerator
Operate the accelerator pedal smoothly and progressively with the right foot.

Clutch
Co-ordinate the use of the clutch pedal with the accelerator or foot brake when moving off, changing gear and stopping. The clutch is used to maintain control over the vehicle when manoeuvring at low speeds in first or reverse gear. Do not drive with your foot resting on or covering the clutch pedal. Avoid coasting, that is keeping the clutch pedal down between gear changes or slipping the gear lever into the neutral position while the car is moving.

Answers to questions on previous pages: 197–a; 198–b; 199–d; 200–a; 201–d; 202–b.

Gears

Check the gear lever is in neutral before starting the engine. Speed up before changing up through the gears, and slow down sufficiently before selecting the correct gear and changing down. Do not look down when you change gear.

Foot brake

Use the mirrors-signal-manoeuvre routine. Operate the foot brake smoothly and progressively to allow the stop lights at the rear of the vehicle to give ample warning to following traffic. Do not drive if the brake lights are not working. Avoid braking on bends and try to slow down when the car is travelling in a straight line. Brake more gently to avoid losing tyre grip and locking the wheels in poor weather conditions. There is a warning light on the dashboard to warn the driver of low brake fluid and if this warning is ignored an accident could result.

Hand brake

Check the hand brake is on before starting the engine, and apply the hand brake before leaving the vehicle. The hand brake should be applied when the car is at a stop junction, waiting at traffic lights, stopped for more than a few seconds, or waiting for pedestrians to cross at a crossing.

Steering

Hold the steering wheel lightly but firmly with both hands unless using one hand for another driving action such as changing gear. Make allowances for the rear wheels to take a short cut when turning to the left. Heavy steering could indicate the tyres are under inflated and this would affect braking and tyre wear as well as steering.

4. Move away

Move off smoothly without endangering other road users. Check in the mirrors and look round to make sure there are no other road users in blind spots not covered by the mirrors.

5. Stop the vehicle in an emergency

The examiner will explain the procedure to you when the vehicle is stationary. When the emergency stop signal is given react promptly and stop the car quickly in a straight line, allowing for road and weather conditions. Hold the steering wheel firmly. Brake quickly but progressively without locking the wheels. Do not push the clutch pedal down until the car has nearly stopped. When the vehicle has stopped apply the hand brake and put the gear lever into neutral.

If the wheels begin to lock during braking, release the brake pedal and re-apply more gently after the wheels have started turning again. The examiner confirms the exercise will not be repeated.

6. Reverse into a limited opening

You may remove the seat belt when reversing. Before reversing look all round the vehicle and wait for pedestrians who are crossing the road, and approaching traffic. Keep the car moving smoothly and be extra careful at the point of turn into the side road when the front of the car will swing out and could endanger passing vehicles. Check to the front and rear and continue to reverse only if safe. For accurate straightening up keep looking through the rear window some distance along the side road and correct mistakes promptly.

7. Turn in the road

Choose a safe place to stop. This manoeuvre is not a 'three point turn' but you should make as few turns as possible. Turn the steering wheel briskly to the right when driving forwards and steer left when reversing. On nearing the kerb, re-position the wheels for the next stage of the turn. Keep the car moving smoothly and do not beckon to other road users or pedestrians, or let your vehicle overhang the pavement. Look all round to check the road is clear during each stage of the turn, and give way to vehicles cyclists and pedestrians unless they wait for you and it is safe to proceed.

8. Reverse park

Stop alongside the chosen vehicle and check all round for traffic and pedestrians before reversing. When it is clear, reverse smoothly and steer to the left until the car is heading in the direction of the kerb. Straighten the wheels and then steer to the right. Stop when the car is parallel and close to the kerb. Correct if necessary by shunting forward and backward.

9. Make effective use of mirrors

Look in the mirrors frequently and treat the interior rear view mirror as a third eye. Use the mirrors-signal-manoeuvre routine and remember all mirrors have blind spots. Use the mirrors before:

Signalling
Look in the mirrors well before signalling. Decide if a signal is necessary and when to give it.

Changing direction
Check mirrors before moving off, turning left or right, before overtaking moving or parked vehicles, before changing lanes and before any other change of direction.

Changing speed
Use the mirrors before slowing or stopping except in an emergency when there is not time. The speed and distance of following traffic will affect the rate at which speed can be reduced safely.

10. Give signals

Where necessary
Signals should be given to help or warn other road users. Thought should be given to the information a signal conveys to another driver and when doubt exists such as turning right after passing a parked car, the indicator signal can be reinforced with an arm signal.

Correctly
Use the indicator or arm signals given in the Highway

Code and cancel signals promptly when a manoeuvre is completed. Do not flash car headlights at other drivers unless to warn them of your presence and do not beckon to pedestrians to cross the road possibly into danger from other vehicles.

Properly timed
Signal in good time but not too early when junctions are close together.

11. Take appropriate action on all:

Traffic signs
Act correctly on the warning or order given by road signs.

Road markings
Road markings are a valuable source of information. The centre line road markings will increase in length and be closer together to warn of hazards. The more white paint, the more hazardous the situation.

Traffic lights
Anticipate traffic lights can change quickly and watch for temporary traffic lights that may be partially obscured by road works.

Signals by traffic controllers
Signals given by police officers, traffic wardens and school crossing patrols showing a 'STOP CHILDREN' sign must be obeyed.

Signals by other road users

Watch for signals given by other road users and act promptly. Use your judgement and be extra careful when people are in charge of animals such as horses, sheep or cattle.

12. Exercise proper care in use of speed

Observe speed limits and take into account road and weather conditions.

Speed limits in mph				
Vehicle	Built-up areas	Single carriageways	Dual carriageways	Motorways
Cars	30	60	70	70
Cars towing	30	50	60	60

13. Keep a safe distance behind vehicles

Follow vehicles at a safe distance and at higher speeds use the two second rule. Wait until the vehicle in front has passed a marker such as a sign or bridge and say "Only a fool breaks the two second rule". You should not pass the marker before you have finished saying the safety rhyme.

Another rule is to leave one metre for each mile per hour you are travelling on the open road; for example at 66 mph leave 66 metres.

Stopping distances

20 mph	=	12 metres	=	3 car lengths
30 mph	=	23 metres	=	6 car lengths
40 mph	=	36 metres	=	9 car lengths
50 mph	=	53 metres	=	13 car lengths
60 mph	=	73 metres	=	18 car lengths
70 mph	=	96 metres	=	24 car lengths

Thinking and braking distances

20 mph	=	6 metres thinking	+	6 metres braking
30 mph	=	9 metres thinking	+	14 metres braking
40 mph	=	12 metres thinking	+	24 metres braking
50 mph	=	15 metres thinking	+	38 metres braking
60 mph	=	18 metres thinking	+	55 metres braking
70 mph	=	21 metres thinking	+	75 metres braking

These distances must be doubled in wet weather and are increased ten times in icy weather.

14. Make progress by:

Driving at a speed appropriate to road and traffic conditions

Your vehicle should not impede the flow of other traffic. Keep up to speed limits when conditions are favourable.

Avoiding undue hesitancy

Do not wait or dither at road junctions or where traffic is waiting to drive on.

15. Act properly at road junctions with regard to:

Speed on approach
Slow to a safe speed. At 'stop' junctions all drivers must stop and give way but at 'give way' junctions stop only if the way is not clear.

Observation
Look both ways and all round before moving into or crossing any junction. If the view is restricted edge forward until you can see and assess the situation. Watch for pedestrians, cyclists and motorcyclists.

Position before turning right
Take up a position just left of the middle of the road and wait just before the point of turn for oncoming traffic to pass. At one-way streets and dual carriageways the right-hand lane should be used.

Position before turning left
Keep to the left and check for bicycles and motorcycles before turning. Do not turn too early at sharp corners or the nearside wheel could mount the pavement. Use deceleration lanes correctly.

Avoid cutting right-hand corners
Do not steer right too soon or the car may cut across traffic emerging from a side road.

16. Deal with other vehicles safely when:

Overtaking
Do not overtake unless the manoeuvre is necessary,

legal and can be completed safely. Use the position, speed, look routine followed by mirrors, signal, manoeuvre. Repeat as needed and allow a good clearance when overtaking. Wait until you can see the vehicle you have overtaken in your rear view mirror and have checked alongside before pulling in again. Give cyclists space in case they wobble or fall.

Meeting
Watch for narrow places and wait back if there is not space to pass safely. If you are in doubt wait and give way to the approaching traffic.

Crossing their path
Before turning right and crossing the path of traffic, give way if your manoeuvre would cause other road users to slow, swerve or stop. Take extra care when passing nearside to nearside as it may be difficult to see oncoming vehicles. Keep a special watch for cyclists and motorcyclists who are more difficult to see.

17. Position the vehicle correctly:

During normal driving
Drive on the left during normal driving, not in the gutter or the middle of the road.

Exercise lane discipline
Choose the correct lane in good time. Some roads are marked with arrows to give advance warning of lane changes and acceleration or deceleration lanes.

18. Allow adequate clearance to stationary vehicles and obstructions

Look ahead and decide if there is space to pass vehicles or obstructions such as skips safely. If in doubt wait well back. Do not 'shave' the corner of the obstruction and allow adequate clearance in case a vehicle starts to move, a door opens or a child runs out. Wait until you are past the obstruction and there is room to move back safely.

19. Take appropriate action at pedestrian crossings

Pedestrians on a crossing have right of way. Where there is a central refuge treat both halves as a separate crossing. Be prepared to stop when people are waiting to cross and a slowing down arm signal may be given. It is an offence to park on the zig-zag lines or overtake the leading vehicle on the approach.

At a pelican crossing pedestrians on the crossing have right of way when the amber light is flashing. Treat a pelican crossing that is staggered on each side of a central island as two separate crossings.

20. Select a safe position for normal stops

Sometimes the examiner specifies the place to stop and at other times the examiner asks the candidate to stop in a convenient place. Choose a place that is safe, legal and will not cause an obstruction. Stop close to the kerb and parallel to it.

21..Show awareness and anticipation of the actions of road users

Cyclists

When passing cyclists leave one metre for the bicycle and one metre for the cyclist! Cyclists may keep in the left-hand lane cycling round roundabouts to avoid having to change and cross lanes of faster traffic.

Pedestrians

Pedestrians have right of way at road junctions. Never beckon a pedestrian to cross the road. Be especially careful when there are children who may run out suddenly from behind vehicles. On narrow country roads watch out for pedestrians who will be walking facing the oncoming traffic.

Animals

Drive very slowly when passing animals such as horses, cows and sheep, and leave as much room as possible. Never sound the horn! Take extra care going round left-hand bends.

22. Use of ancillary controls

The examiner will expect you to be able to operate the heater, windscreen wipers, demister and other ancillary controls.

DRIVING TUITION

Any person giving tuition in return for payment, even petrol money, must by law display a valid Approved Driving Instructor (ADI) licence. During driving tuition the green licence which contains a photograph of the ADI must be displayed on the windscreen of the tuition vehicle.

Trainee driving instructors

Trainee instructors who have not passed the examination which tests instructional ability must display a pink licence and this is issued for a period of six months only.

Further training

New drivers in the 17–25 years age group are much more likely to be involved in an accident, especially in the first year of driving. After passing the Driving Test new drivers should be advised to take motorway lessons with an ADI before driving on motorways.

DRIVING INSTRUCTOR ASSOCIATIONS

Driving Instructors' Association
Safety House
Beddington Farm Road
Croydon CRO 4XZ

Telephone 0181-665 5151

Motor Schools' Association
182A Heaton Moor Road
Stockport
Cheshire SK4 4DU

Telephone 0161-443 1611